W9-CRP-120

QUEST FOR
THE TREE KANGAROO

QUEST FOR THE TREE KANGAROO

AN EXPEDITION TO THE CLOUD FOREST OF NEW GUINEA

text by SY MONTGOMERY

photographs by NIC BISHOP

sandpiper

Houghton Mifflin Harcourt ◦ Boston New York

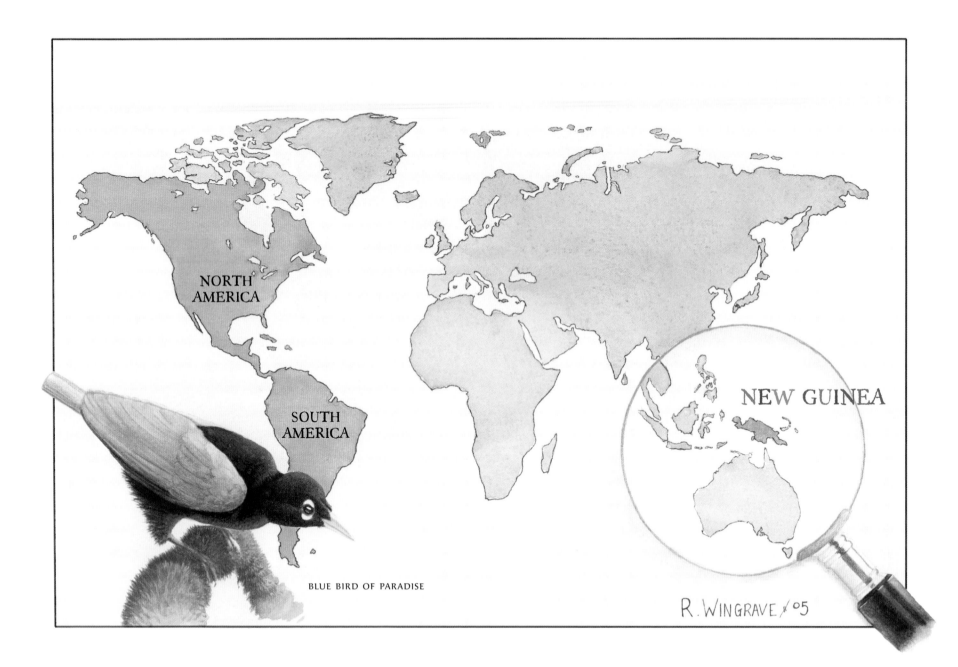

NORTH AMERICA

SOUTH AMERICA

NEW GUINEA

BLUE BIRD OF PARADISE

R. WINGRAVE / 05

PAPUA NEW GUINEA

GREY BELLIED TREE MOUSE

MOUNTAIN CUSCUS

FINISTERRE RANGE

Yawan

Wasaunon

Nadzab Airport

Lae

Huon Gulf

Solomon Sea

NEW GUINEA HARPY EAGLE

OWEN STANLEY RANGE

Gulf of Papua

N

W E

S

Port Moresby

SUGAR GLIDER

0   50   100   150   200 miles

NEW GUINEA PADEMELON

R.WINGRAVE 05

A "BIG STUFFED ANIMAL" ON A STONE AGE ISLAND

IT FEELS LIKE WE'VE WALKED INTO A LIVING FAIRY TALE. OUR HEADS ARE LITERALLY IN THE CLOUDS. THOUGH WE'RE JUST A FEW DEGREES SOUTH OF THE EQUATOR, WE'RE bathed in cool mist. We're 10,000 feet up in the mountains. Here, the trees are cloaked in clouds. The ground is carpeted with thick green moss. In the cloud forest of Papua New Guinea, ferns grow into trees — trees like those the dinosaurs knew. Moss and ferns, vines and orchids, hang from branches like the beards of wise old wizards.

In a place like this, we half expect a hobbit or a troll to show up. But it's better than that. The animals who really *do* live here are even more fantastic — and directly above us is one of them.

"This is incredible!"

Lisa Dabek, forty-five, can't help but exclaim each time she sees one in the wild. She's the scientific leader of our research team, and she's fixed her binoculars on one of the rarest, strangest, and least understood creatures on the planet. More than eighty feet above her, high in one of the tall, ancient trees, a kangaroo is looking down at us.

A *kangaroo* in a *tree?*

That's just what Lisa thought when she met her first tree kangaroo about twenty years ago.

The encounter took place at the Woodland Park Zoo in Seattle, Washington. Lisa was a graduate student in animal behavior. She had never heard of a tree kangaroo before. But meeting one changed her life.

"It looked like a big stuffed animal!" she remembers. Or something that Dr. Seuss might have dreamed up. Impossibly soft, with a rounded face, button eyes, pink nose, pert upright ears and a long thick tail, it was about the size of a small dog or an overweight cat, with plush brown and golden fur.

⌐ *Lisa scans the canopy for tree kangaroos.* ⌐

7

There were two of them—two mothers with tiny babies concealed in their pouches. They were as strange as they were adorable.

"They were like monkeys up in the trees—but they weren't monkeys," she recalls. "They looked a little like bears—but they weren't bears. And then they had a pouch for their babies—a totally different thing from most other mammals."

What she was looking at then—and what we're seeing today above us in the tree—was a Matschie's ("MATCH-eez") tree kangaroo. It's one of ten kinds of tree kangaroos on the planet. "I was totally intrigued," Lisa said. "I fell completely in love with these animals."

Lisa learned at the zoo that the Matschie's tree kangaroo is among the rarest creatures on earth—and getting rarer. As people cut down the cloud forest and killed more and more kangaroos, the species was disappearing.

She decided to do something about it.

And that's what's brought Lisa and us, a team of scientists and volunteers she's gathered from three continents to help her, on this quest to a remote and magical forest in the clouds. We've come to try to learn the secrets of these rare creatures. What do they eat? How many are left? What do they need to survive? We hope to find out the answers—before it's too late.

o o o

The Matschie's live in "a lost world," on "a Stone Age island," in "a land that time forgot." That's how people still describe New Guinea. It's the second-largest island on Earth. Only one island (Greenland) is bigger. Only the Amazon has more tropical rainforest. But New Guinea has many other different habitats for animals to live in besides tropical rainforest—from seashores to coral reefs to glaciers to cloud forests.

New Guinea was mostly unexplored by outsiders until the middle of the twentieth century. And for good reason: the place is full of tangled jungles, steep mountains, erupting volcanoes, dangerous mudslides, aggressive crocodiles, poisonous snakes, and tropical diseases. The few explorers who survived expeditions there noted another hazard: The local people sometimes had newcomers for dinner—literally. Headhunting cannibal tribes sometimes ate people *clothes and all*—except for their shoes. (They gave the shoes to their pigs to eat, just as dogs eat rawhide chews.)

Things have changed. Headhunting fell out of fashion. It's thought that nobody eats people there anymore. But still, especially on the eastern half of the island—the nation known as Papua New Guinea—few roads mar the wilderness. Ancient forests remain unexplored. New species are still being found.

Here you'll find birds that grow as tall as a man. Cassowaries remind you of dinosaurs. They sport tall helmets of bone growing up from their blue and black heads. Long, skinny black feathers hang from their bodies like hair. Because they have only tiny stumps for wings, cassowaries can't fly. But they sure can fight! They can leap into the air and slash at their enemies with claws as sharp as razors. Other birds—like the pitohui ("PIT-oh-whee")—have *poisonous feathers*. And still others are so beautiful, they are called birds of paradise.

Strange animals abound. The triok ("TREE-okk") is a beautiful black and white striped possum with a pink nose and huge black eyes. The fourth finger on each hand is more than twice as long as the others—all the better to fish grubs from holes in rotting trees.

The echidna ("eee-KID-nah") is a spine-covered, worm-eating mammal who lays eggs instead of giving birth to live babies. The dorcopsis ("door-COP-sis") is a fat little kangaroo who grows no longer than your forearm. The pademelon ("PAD-e-melon") is another, who sleeps in soft beds of grass. The cuscus ("CUSS-cuss") lives in trees. Its eyes are huge, its fur thick and soft. It holds on to branches with pink hands and a pink grasping tail.

But perhaps the most amazing of them all is the Matschie's tree kangaroo. It lives only in one place in the world: the cloud forest of the Huon Peninsula, on the northeast coast of Papua New Guinea. (The western half of New Guinea is part of the much larger nation of Indonesia.)

New Guinea isn't exactly the sort of place you'd expect a typical kid growing up in a New York City apartment to end up . . . but Lisa wasn't typical.

○ ○ ○

Lisa always loved animals—watching them, reading about them, writing stories about them. But being with animals wasn't easy. She was so allergic to fur, she even had to give away her beloved cat, Twinkles, when she was eleven. She couldn't have a dog, either.

As a child, sometimes she would wake at night gasping for breath. Lisa has asthma. She loved sports, but she couldn't join the track or basketball teams. (Sometimes running made her breathing worse.) Who'd have thought she'd grow up to be a tree kangaroo scientist, climbing 10,000-foot mountains into the thin air of the cloud forest?

Not Lisa's elementary school teachers. Since kindergarten, not one of them encouraged her interest in animals. In fact, one teacher complained to Lisa's mother—she thought a little girl who always wrote stories about animals was odd.

Lisa's two older sisters weren't as excited about animals as Lisa was. But their mom, the principal at a nursery school, understood. She loved animals and nature, too.

How could Lisa bring animals into her life? Living in New York City, how could she observe them in the wild? "We didn't have a lawn or a backyard," Lisa remembers. "Instead, we had the asphalt roof of the garage." Even there, she found a way. Little ants lived on the roof. So Lisa decided to study them. She used to collect them in Dixie cups—that way she could

— Matschie's tree kangaroos enjoy the leaves of trees, ferns, and orchids. —

pick them up without hurting them—and watch whatever they did. (Mainly they tried to get out of the cup.) Then she would let them go.

Later, in high school, Lisa researched a report on beluga whales, the beautiful white whales of the Arctic. She read books and articles. But that wasn't enough. She went to the New York Aquarium. She decided to see what she could find out by watching the beluga whales "up close and personal." She even got to touch one.

The next year, as a senior, Lisa volunteered to help a scientist at the American Museum of Natural History in New York. He was studying electric fish. One really big electric fish lived in a tank in his lab. She remembers that he told her to put her hand in the tank—to feel how strong the shock was. "I was a little scared, but I did it," she said. "And I felt it! It was a strong shock, but it didn't hurt. And I thought, *wow,* this is *amazing*—and so is this whole world of learning about animals."

o o o

In college, and as a graduate student, Lisa studied wild elephant seals and sea lions in California. (When she was outdoors, fur didn't trigger her allergies.) She studied titi monkeys and squirrel monkeys in a primate center at the University of California, Davis. But when she met her first tree kangaroos at Seattle's Woodland Park Zoo, she knew they were special. She knew that she would be willing to do anything to help these endangered animals. And she knew what she would have to do next.

You guessed it. Lisa began traveling to the Huon Peninsula. Most of the time she was based at the Roger Williams Park Zoo in Providence, Rhode Island. There are tree kangaroos there, and she worked as the zoo's director of conservation and research. Every year she would make a trip to Papua New Guinea to try to see the tree kangaroos in the wild.

Lisa made expedition after expedition. The mountain hikes were hard.

She carried an inhaler to help her breathe. She took special pills to open her airways. But over the years, she had built up her strength. And in Papua New Guinea, she was in for a wonderful surprise: Even though the air was thin at 10,000 feet, it was pure. America's air pollution made Lisa's asthma worse; New Guinea's clean air made it better!

For weeks, working with local trackers and a field assistant from home, she'd comb the mountains. Many times she thought she saw a tail or the hunched body of a tree kangaroo looking down at her. But it was only a clump of moss.

In a five-week expedition in 1996, she saw two tree kangaroos—one of whom she glimpsed so briefly she got only a single photo. The other she was able to watch for forty-five minutes, and videotape.

But then she didn't see another—for seven years.

No wonder. To most tree kangaroos, people are frightening enemies. With bow and arrow, sometimes with the help of dogs, people have hunted and eaten them for hundreds of years. As more Matschie's tree kangaroos were killed, the ones who were left grew more afraid. The minute they'd hear Lisa coming, they'd hide. But the tree kangaroos' fear only increased her determination to help them.

At the villages in the mountains, Lisa and her growing team met with local landowners. The team and the landowners spoke together about the disappearing tree kangaroos. After meeting with the conservationists, the people agreed to set aside some of their land as no-hunting zones. This land would be a sort of "wildlife bank" where the animals could live in peace.

Lisa and her team also talked with local schoolteachers. Lisa wanted the kids to learn how lucky they were to have tree kangaroos and echidnas, cuscus and trioks. She wanted them to understand how important it is to protect the forest.

Meanwhile, Lisa tried to learn about the tree kangaroos—even though she couldn't see them. How? With assistants who stayed in the field, she studied their small oval dark green droppings—the people call it "pek pek" —to try to see what the tree kangaroos were eating. They tried to guess how many animals lived there. She and the team looked for scratch marks on the trees where the animals' claws had dug into the moss-covered bark. They talked to local people, who told Lisa what they had learned from hunting the creatures.

o o o

Then, in late 2003, everything changed. Lisa found out about a place where the tree kangaroos hadn't been hunted in many years. In fact, no tree kangaroo living there was old enough to remember hunters. (In captivity, a tree kangaroo can live as long as a cat, sometimes even into their twenties.) They had little fear of people.

And that's where we're standing now. We're hoping we can capture this beautiful tree kangaroo, just for a short time. We hope to outfit it with a radio collar. By following the radio signal with telemetry equipment, we want to track the animal through the dense forest—even when we can't see it. This way we can learn and we can help.

We are so full of questions. Can we get the kangaroo down from the tree? Catch it before it gets away? Safely collar the animal? And if we do, will the collar stay on and work?

Will our team be able to follow the signal? Will tree kangaroos show us what they need to survive so we can help protect them? Or will the lives of these mysterious animals remain secret forever?

Other scientists have told Lisa that tracking tree kangaroos is impossible.

But we've got to try.

THE ADVENTURE BEGINS

To join Lisa on her tree kangaroo expedition, we've come from all over the world. Lisa has gathered scientists from Massachusetts, from England, and from Papua New Guinea. An artist came from Australia. A veterinarian flew in from Seattle. A zookeeper came from Minnesota. All of us have different talents we hope to use to help the tree kangaroos—as you'll see when you meet our team:

HOLLY REED, forty-eight, is our field veterinarian. Working at Point Defiance Zoo and Aquarium in Washington State, she's done a root canal on a polar bear's teeth, removed a tumor from an aardvark, and even treated a kind of sea horse, known as a leafy sea dragon, for an infected swim bladder. (The swim bladder helps fish float. Holly had to make a special life preserver to keep the sea dragon afloat while he got better.) But this is her most exciting opportunity yet.

CHRISTINE MCKNIGHT, thirty-six, originally planned

LEFT: The eclectus parrot is common in New Guinea. This is a female; the male is bright green. FACING: Green tree pythons are common in lowland forest.

to be a medical doctor—but then she got an internship at the Minnesota Zoo. Now she works with some of the zoo's coolest animals: clouded leopards, who are great tree climbers; beautiful, fluffy long-tailed civets called binturongs from Southeast Asia; and even Malaysian tapirs—rainforest-dwellers that look like a cross between an elephant, a pig, and a horse. But the rarest of them all, her favorites, are the Matschie's tree kangaroos.

GABRIEL POROLAK, twenty-seven, is a graduate student and one of Lisa's two field scientists. He's been studying the tree kangaroos up in the cloud forest since 2002. Gabriel grew up loving animals. As a kid, he had two pet grasshoppers, a gecko lizard, a parrot, a cat, a dog, and a pigeon named Bozo that he raised from an egg he found in the gutter of a roof. But even though he's a native of Papua New Guinea, he never saw a wild Matschie's tree kangaroo until he worked with Lisa. "I fell in love at first sight," he said. "You should hold one—you would never want to let it go! And you would want to do anything and everything to help this animal."

JOEL GLICK, twenty-eight, grew up in Massachusetts, but ever since elementary school he wanted to study mountain gorillas in Africa. He spent two years in Uganda doing just that. He's also studied monkeys all over the world. Joel's used to climbing mountains, watching animals up in the trees, and camping out—and that's why Lisa hired him as her field coordinator/scientist for the Tree Kangaroo Conservation Program. With Gabriel and a staff of native trackers, Joel lived in the cloud forest for a whole year.

Now Joel's back, to help train the new field coordinator,

TOBY ROSS, twenty-nine. Toby's from England, with a master's degree earned in studying reptiles. Working with a rare sort of lizard, the orange-tailed skink (only discovered in 1995), he learned how to solve the mysteries of the most elusive animals. In 2004, Toby caught and studied 120 of them, and discovered for the first time where they live, how fast they grow, and what they eat. Toby will take over where Joel left off.

ROBIN WINGRAVE, thirty-six, is the artist who painted the maps in this book and the animals and plants on them. Robin lives in Australia. While he was working in a resort hotel there, he went along on a tour company's nighttime nature expeditions. While shining spotlights into trees, he discovered "there was a whole world of life up there that nobody knew about." Robin bought the gear he needed to climb into the trees and explore them himself—and paint what he found. "From my artwork," he says, "it's my hope that people get a new appreciation of the unique ecosystem that's here in Papua New Guinea."

Doria's tree kangaroo lives in the central mountain ranges of New Guinea.

NIC BISHOP, forty-nine, took all the photos in this book. An author, photographer, and biologist, Nic was born in England and is a citizen of New Zealand. Now he lives in Michigan. But he once lived in Papua New Guinea. When Nic was fourteen, his family moved there so his dad could work as a teacher with the United Nations. Nic loved to explore the bush with the family's Papuan gardener. This will be Nic's first time back in the country since he left when he was nearly eighteen.

And there's me. I'm SY MONTGOMERY, forty-seven. I wrote the words in this book. I met Lisa when she was director of conservation and research at the Roger Williams Park Zoo in Providence, Rhode Island, in the year 2000—before she moved to Seattle's Woodland Park Zoo. I'd been hoping to visit her project in Papua New Guinea ever since.

o o o

All of us prepared for the trip carefully. We all got shots to prevent tropical diseases. We brought pills to protect us from malaria. We stuffed our backpacks with rain gear and fleece jackets, water bottles and bug repellent. We've got hiking boots and sleeping bags, flashlights and walking sticks, clothespins and safety pins, lip balm and Band-Aids.

But our personal gear is just the beginning. For our two-week expedition, we'll also need food for ourselves and the local people who will help us. We'll need tents to live in, pots and pans to cook with, scientific and veterinary supplies. Under Lisa's guidance, Gabriel and Joel bought and organized it all in advance.

So besides our luggage, here's what's going to go on the twelve-seat Twin Otter propeller plane that will take us from the Papuan city of Lae to our first stop, the village of Yawan:

- 20 liters of kerosene
- 5 cardboard boxes filled with pasta, peanut butter, tomato paste, cookies, lentils, jam, popcorn, pesto, soy sauce, and dried fruit
- 4 bales of sugar
- 7 cartons of crackers
- 3 bales of rice
- 2 cartons of canned fish
- 2 cartons of corned beef
- 1 carton of canned chicken
- 6 boxes of dishwashing detergent
- 6 kilograms of salt
- 6 two-liter cans of cooking oil
- 3 five-liter containers of ethanol, to preserve scientific specimens like kangaroo dung
- 10 big white bags full of chairs, batteries, and scientific equipment (radio collars, telemetry receivers, Global Positioning System units), veterinary supplies, solar panels, and satellite phone
- 3 big, hard-sided suitcases
- 3 large backpacks with other supplies
- 48 rolls of toilet paper

We hope it will all fit. We're at the cement and cinderblock airport in Lae, with all the supplies, by seven A.M., ready to leave.

And we're still there at noon.

"The whole area is really cloudy," Lisa tells us after checking with the

Mission Aviation Fellowship office. "But they're going to try to get us to Yawan later this afternoon."

Ours isn't a regular flight, like you would take to visit your aunt or to go to Disneyland. Mission Aviation Fellowship planes are operated by missionaries, and the pilots are on a different schedule each day. Our plane has five other stops before it gets to us. Clouds—and what else would you expect in a cloud forest?—can ruin the whole schedule. Once Joel was stuck in a remote village for *three weeks* waiting for a plane.

Ten airstrips at different destinations are closed on this particular day. Clouds aren't the only problem. One airstrip doesn't have a wind sock, so the pilot can't tell which way the wind is blowing. Two others are closed because the grass on the runway is too long. (Nobody has a lawn mower in the village. People trim the grass with their bush knives.)

Finally, the Twin Otter comes at 2:30 P.M. The weather is OK in Lae, but it's not so good around Yawan, the pilot says. We're going to try to fly anyway. If the clouds are bad, he might have to fly

Lisa and the team on the flight in.
FACING PAGE: Yawan village and airstrip,
seen from the climb up to the field site.

above 14,000 feet—to make sure the plane doesn't crash into the mountains. At heights like that, the air is thin. "Does anybody have breathing problems?" the pilot asks. Both Lisa and Toby raise their hands. Toby has asthma, too.

"We'll keep an oxygen bottle nearby," the pilot tells us. He points out the air sickness bags. What else could go wrong? (We don't even want to think about it . . .) And, at last, at 3:25 P.M. we're off.

We rise through the air, leaving the city behind. Soon there are no roads below us. No houses. Then a few villages, with thatched roofs and small gardens. Clouds. Mountains. A rainbow.

The spines of the tree-clad mountains look as jagged as the back of a stegosaurus. The pilot turns our plane sharply. We see a beautiful waterfall to our right, and small, neat handmade houses thatched with palms. It's Yawan village. We land at 3:50 P.M. Everyone applauds. We made it.

than any other place of comparable size on Earth.

A huge portion of the plants and animals found here live nowhere else: 60 percent of its more than 11,000 kinds of plants, more than 400 species of its birds, and at least 60 species of its mammals live only here. And there are many other kinds of critters, too—many of them unique. Scientists have counted more than 300 species of freshwater fish, more than 200 kinds of frogs, and more than 300 different reptiles on this island—and they're still counting!

One reason New Guinea's plants and animals are unique is that these creatures evolved in isolation, away from the big land masses of Asia and Australia. But the reason these animals survived is that no one has ruined their homes—yet. New Guinea is one of the wildest, leafiest spots left on the planet. Forests cover 65 percent of the island. In the United States, forests cover less than half the land. Unfortunately in West Papua—owned by the nation of

New Guinea is both the longest and the highest tropical island in the world. And there's plenty more that's special about the place:

The island boasts the world's largest pigeon, the world's smallest parrot, its biggest butterfly and the its longest lizard. New Guinea has more orchid species Indonesia—much of the forest has been razed for timber and for gold mines. But the picture is much better in the independent nation of Papua New Guinea. There, 90 percent of the land is still forested. Conservationists consider it one of the great biological jewels of the world.

— *Victoria crowned pigeon, the world's largest pigeon.* —

MARSUPIAL MANIA

Stewart Little, the small mouse with big parents, had nothing on baby marsupials. Marsupials ("mar-SOUP-ee-ulz") are special kinds of mammals. Even the biggest ones give birth to babies who are incredibly small. A 200-pound, six-foot mother kangaroo, for instance, gives birth to a baby as small as a lima bean. That's what makes marsupials marsupials. Their babies are born so tiny that in order to survive, they must live in a pouch on the mother's tummy. The pouch is called a marsupium. (Don't you wish *you* had one?)

A baby marsupial lives hidden in the mother's warm, moist pouch for months. There it sucks milk from a nipple like other baby mammals. One day it's big enough to poke its head out to see the world. The European explorers who saw kangaroos for the first time in Australia reported they had discovered a two-headed animal—with one head on the neck and another on the belly.

North America only has one marsupial. You may have seen it: The Virginia opossum actually lives in most of the United States, not just Virginia. South America also has marsupials. But most marsupials live in or near Australia. They include the koala (which is *not* a bear), two species of wombat, the toothy black Tasmanian devil, four species of black-and-white spotted "native cats" (though they're not cats at all), and many others.

The most famous marsupials, however, are the kangaroos. All kangaroos hop—some of them six feet high and faster than forty miles an hour. More than fifty different species of kangaroo hop around on the ground—from the big red kangaroo to the one-pound musky rat kangaroo.

Few people know that there are ten more species of kangaroo who have taken to the trees. Tree kangaroos hop, too. Unlike regular kangaroos, they can also climb —although sometimes they look a bit unsteady. They use sharp claws on the front feet to grip branches. And they can move their hind legs independently of one another—something regular kangaroos can't do.

Two tree kangaroo species live in Australia. Eight live in New Guinea. At least that's how many species scientists have found so far. A new one—a black and white tree kangaroo called a Dingiso ("den-GEE-so")—was discovered as recently as 1995.

Lumholtz's tree kangaroo is found in Queensland, Australia.

PARTNERS IN CONSERVATION

Yawan is a beautiful village. A huge waterfall flows down a green mountain. The people have planted colorful gardens around their houses. Each house is built about a foot and a half off the ground on stilts—convenient protection from floods and unwanted visits from animals. Banana trees grow in the yards.

About eighty people from the village are waiting on the grass landing strip to greet Lisa and our team. A village leader steps forward. His name is Dono, and he and Lisa have been friends for years. "Welcome to Yawan," he says to us all in English.

Most people here don't speak English, but they speak at least two other languages. One is Tok Pisin. Almost all the people in Papua New Guinea speak it. Tok Pisin is made up of bits of other languages, including English. If you say words written in Tok Pisin out loud, you will probably recognize many of them. (Tok Pisin itself sounds like "Talk Pidgin.") And most people in Papua New Guinea also speak a language unique to their village. In Tok Pisin, these individual village languages are called Tok Ples

ABOVE: Gosing is Lisa's "adopted aunt" and accompanies her each year on the walk to the field site. FACING PAGE: Supplies and expedition members off load at Yawan airstrip.

25

(it sounds like "Talk Place"). On the island of New Guinea, more than a thousand different languages are spoken. That's one sixth of all the languages in the *world*.

The elders hug Lisa and shake our hands to welcome us. Many of the women have small blue or black tattoos on their faces—a set of small shining suns on the cheeks, or a series of upright lines on the forehead. Children rush up to greet us, smiling but a little shy. Dono's thirteen-year-old daughter, Melchy, is particularly eager to see Lisa. She's waiting for a letter from her penpal, Lisa's nine-year-old niece, Nadja—and of course Lisa remembered to bring the envelope.

The people of Yawan, along with their neighbors in nearby villages, are our partners in conservation. Without them, explains Lisa, "none of this would be happening. Nothing we are doing would work at all." And yet, not long ago, many of them hunted tree kangaroos. Almost everyone ate them. They almost ate every last one.

Yawit, an elder wearing a big leather hat, told me about those days. Once Yawit was a champion tree kangaroo hunter. He has killed at least a thousand. He used to chase them with dogs and shoot them with his bow and arrows. His neighbors were impressed. They all liked tree kangaroo meat. They used the fur—especially the tail—to make fancy headdresses. Sometimes, Yawit remembers, he would kill five or ten tree kangaroos in a single day.

But now he has stopped killing. A few years before Lisa arrived, missionaries came to Yawan. The people believed in forest spirits; the missionaries believed in Jesus. The missionaries gave the people many handy things like antibiotic medicines and ready-made clothing, and invited them to join their church. They were Seventh-day Adventists. Their church preached that people should eat only the foods permitted in the Old Testament (and nobody in Israel was eating tree kangaroos when the Bible was being written). When Yawit joined the church, he stopped hunting to obey its rules. (Most villagers now eat chickens instead.) Since Yawit met Lisa, he's especially glad he stopped hunting; he understands that too much hunting could mean no tree kangaroos left at all. "Now I just turn and watch them do whatever they want," he said, as Gabriel translated. "I appreciate seeing them. Now, I am bound by two laws: one by the church, and one by conservation."

Tidy thatch houses are surrounded by gardens and flowers.

Schoolteacher Pekison announces roll call with a triton shell "trumpet."

Conservation made so much sense to the local people that landowners decided to donate some of their land to protect the tree kangaroos. Our research site is within that conservation area. So far, landowners have pledged more than 100,000 acres of cloud forest for tree kangaroo conservation—an area about seven times the size of Manhattan.

A couple of years ago, village elders honored Lisa with a special ceremony. They presented all the village's bows and arrows and spears to her. "You take them," they said. "We don't need them anymore."

∘ ∘ ∘

Lisa's friends in the village will also be our partners and guides at the field site. Without them, we could never find the tree kangaroos. We could never even get our food and gear up the mountain.

The twenty liters of kerosene, the seventeen cartons of food, the three large backpacks, the four bales of sugar, the three bales of rice, the salt, the detergent, the oil, the chairs and clothes and batteries and scientific and veterinary supplies that came on the plane—all that *plus* ten tents, two teapots, plates, knives, forks, spoons, pans, and all the fresh vegetables we can eat— will have to be *carried* to our field site. There are no cars. There are no roads. The only way to get there is to hike.

It'll take us three days.

Much of our gear will be packed into big white burlap sacks. Some of us find these hard to lift, much less carry. But most local people are so strong that they can easily carry more than thirty pounds all day long. Even children as young as nine can carry more than twenty pounds. But we still need lots of people to help.

Including our team from abroad, along with our porters and trackers and in some cases their families, forty-four people will hike up the mountain—including two babies, one toddler, and a number of kids from ages six to sixteen. Who knows—maybe one of those kids will grow up to be a tree kangaroo scientist one day!

"I really believe the future of conservation is with kids," Lisa says. "The more kids around the world understand the importance of protecting plants and animals, the better off we'll be." That's why one of the first things Lisa did when she came to work in the villages was to set up conservation education programs in the schools—as we discover the very next morning.

Schoolteacher Pekison Kusso doesn't ring a school bell to signal the start of classes. Instead, he blows into a triton shell, which sounds like a high-pitched foghorn. All the kids come running.

Lucky for us, it's Wednesday. That's "wear your traditional clothes to school day" in Yawan. Ready-made clothes are now easily available, but teachers like Pekison don't want the kids to forget the barkcloth outfits their parents and grandparents wore.

The boys sport short pants and long capes handmade from the brown bark of the pandanus palm. The girls wear bark cloth capes, too, as well as skirts made of dried grass, and look very pretty.

The kids take their seats at their desks; some sit on woven mats on the floor. Today they are drawing rainforest animals. A seven-year-old is drawing a tree kangaroo. He tells us through Gabriel, "When I see a tree kangaroo, I'm excited. Even seeing a picture of one makes me happy!" At the desk next to him, a classmate is coloring in red and pink flowers on his drawing of cloud forest plants.

Pekison believes that conservation is a subject just as important as math or reading. If we don't learn how to conserve, the teacher explains, we could lose everything—the tree kangaroos, the forests, even the vines to build houses. "But because we teach conservation," he says, "children will grow up finding it easy to conserve in the future."

To help students learn how to protect the wild world around them, the Tree Kangaroo Conservation Program raised money for school supplies. Teachers at Roger Williams Park Zoo and the Columbus Zoo in Ohio wrote lesson plans. Kids in the United States and Australia exchanged drawings of wildlife with kids from the villages. Lisa organized U.S. zoos to fund scholarships to train teachers and to send students to college.

Nine-year-old Ali says through Gabriel that he thinks tree kangaroos are so beautiful that no one should hunt them. And then Gabriel tells him an important fact: "These kangaroos are found only here. Nowhere else. Not anywhere else in Papua New Guinea. Not in Africa or Europe or America."

The boy's dark eyes widen. What does Ali think of that?

"It's good it's found only here," he decides. "Our place has something special. Something we can be proud of."

° ° °

The people of the Huon Peninsula have much to be proud of—and much to share with us. After our busy morning with the kids, two of the elders offer us a special treat. As our send-off from Yawan, they're going to perform a traditional song and dance.

Joshua Nimoniong and Bonyepe Dingya dress in ceremonial clothes made of barkcloth. They darken their eyes with black charcoal. They paint their faces and bodies with splashes of white ash.

"The color white reflects what comes from our hearts," Joshua explains as Gabriel translates. In Tok Pisin, Gabriel says, the word for this heartfelt feeling is "one-man." In painting their bodies with white, Joshua and Bonyepe are showing that Yawan's people and our team are all in this together. And topping it all off, the men wear spectacular necklaces—cowrie shells and dog teeth—and even more spectacular hats.

Both hats are made of bamboo frames. Both are decorated with the bright red feathers of the female eclectus parrot and the tall, dark feathers of the hornbill. And both hats have moving parts. The feathers are attached to springs—so as the men dip their knees to dance, the feathers rock back and forth, as if they are dancing, too. "It makes others want to join in the dance," Joshua explains.

The two men dance and sing and beat out the rhythm to their song on their kundu drums. The beat, the melody, the moving hats—it *does* make you want to join in. But what is the song about?

Joshua explains: "The song is about going into the bush," he tells us through Gabriel. "It's about the flowers, the trees, the mosses, and about appreciating and respecting them. It's an old song we sing when we go into the forest. It helps us keep our thoughts on the forest."

Our thoughts are on the forest, too. For this afternoon, we begin the first leg of our three-day hike into the cloud forest. Joshua will be one of the local people coming along.

Our first day's hike is just a couple of hours. But it's hard—the slope is steep and muddy. On this night, we'll sleep in our sleeping bags inside a house on stilts in the pretty village of Towet. The real challenge will come the next day. A steep nine-hour hike will take us far from the villages . . . and up into the misty mountains of the Matschie's tree kangaroos.

THE HIKE TO HEAVEN

Lisa tells us that the first three hours are the worst. She's right. Oxygen gets thinner the higher we climb. Some of us find it hard to breathe. The muddy slopes are slippery and steep. To pull ourselves up, we grab roots and vines.

We start along an open ridge. The sun beats down, hot. Sweat pours off our faces. Bugs swarm, sip our sweat, suck our blood. But we hardly notice. All that matters is the next step: how to get one foot from *here* to *there*.

Each step offers a new opportunity for disaster: Sliding backwards in the greasy mud. Crashing down a hole. Slipping on a slick log. And then there's the bridge over the river . . . best not to look down.

There are also stinging nettles that the locals call "fire plants." Tiny black leeches can brush off the tips of leaves and onto our skin. The locals call the leech "rubber snake." Leeches aren't snakes, of course. But just as some snakes have venom, leeches have chemicals in their drool. One chemical acts as a local anesthetic—that's why you can have a leech on you and never know it. Leeches feed on blood until they're full and fall off. On a previous expedition, a leech dropped into Lisa's *eye. Yuck!* The field vet removed it with tweezers.

But we're too busy to watch out for leeches or nettles. We hardly even notice the beautiful view. "When you hike in New Guinea," says Lisa, "what you see is the ground." We watch for the place where strong, bare toes squeezed into the mud—the footprints of our local partners ahead of us, carrying our gear.

To get in shape for this hike, many of us Westerners worked out at health clubs. We brought good hiking shoes. We're taking special vitamins. Yet in terms of overall fitness—strength, endurance—the local people, in their bare feet, leave us Westerners in the dust. Or the mud.

ABOVE: Leeches are just one of the discomforts of New Guinea hiking. FACING: This year-old bridge was built from saplings lashed together with vines after a flood destroyed the last one.

Except they *don't* leave us behind. Though most of the porters and trackers are far ahead, some stay with us. Gosing, one of Lisa's favorite women friends from Yawan village, turns to encourage Lisa and check on the rest of us. Even though Gosing is an elder, for her these slopes are easy. Lisa gives her a big smile. A number of other village women are quietly looking after us. They know when to lend a hand when a member of the team needs help. When we fall, they help us up. We laugh together. The hike is hard work, but our new friends make it fun.

○ ○ ○

We pause after three hours at the top of a ridge. We've made it through the hardest part. Here, we learn, a thirty-year-old graduate student on a previous team, a guy so strong he was a bodybuilder, threw up and declared he could go no farther. (He eventually made it, though.) We sit and sip water and share PowerBars and chocolate cookies.

The scene below takes our breath away. Down, down, down stretches the slope we just climbed. Down, down, down we look, into the people's gardens. Far away, as if we are looking down from the airplane again, the villages look tiny. We seem to have climbed an impossible distance. But we are still, our Papuan friends tell us, "longwe" (long way) from our destination. We're

not even "longwe lik-lik" (which means little long way)—and certainly not "klostu" our field site. Before we camp for the night, six more hours of hiking remain. And then three more in the morning before we reach our research camp.

○ ○ ○

We do it in three-hour chunks. Now we head along a ridge toward the Yapum River. Here we find "houseplants" growing wild on the ground. We recognize plants from the pots on our windowsills at home: the reddish ridged leaves of Coleus; the white blooms of New Guinea impatiens.

We're also seeing more moss on the ground. We are entering a higher, wilder area. At about two-thirty Lisa points out a special plant. It looks like a young raspberry bush, but with no spines. "When you see this," she says, "you know you're in tree kangaroo country."

Everywhere around us now is almost blinding beauty. Great trees hung with moss. Tree ferns with coiled leaf buds bigger than cabbages. The higher we climb, the tree trunks grow fatter, the forest cooler, moister, and mistier.

"Can we hike another three hours?" Lisa asks our group.

We agree that we can. The plan is to meet the porters at the Kotem River, where we'll camp for the night. But first we'll have to complete the final third of our nine-hour hike—a very steep, difficult walk downhill to the river.

Hazards lurk everywhere. "Hole!" calls Lisa. "Pass it down!" We've got an early-warning system to alert those behind. "Really slippery rock!" warns Lisa. "Rotten logs!" calls Holly. "Bad mud!" cries Christine.

When we finally do arrive, it's near dark. The sky opens and it begins to pour. Thoughtfully, our village friends, having arrived earlier, have made a canopy for us. A series of blue tarps, mounted on poles cut from saplings and tied with vines, will keep us dry like a giant umbrella. Beneath this canopy we can pitch our tents without getting wetter than we already are. Someone has made a campfire and is boiling water for our dinner of rice and greens.

Two to a tent, we sleep to the rhythm of rain.

WELCOME TO THE CLOUD FOREST

"Look—I'm SpongeBob WetPants!" Toby could be speaking for all of us. In the morning, everything is soaked. We pull on wet socks, wet pants, wet shoes. We pack our tents. We refill our water bottles from the clean, cool river. Today's hike should take only three hours. But most of it is uphill.

As we make our way up, some of the porters are coming down. We shake hands and say "tenk yu tru"—thank you true. We bid goodbye to many of those who carried our food and our tents, our scientific and veterinary supplies.

After two hours, we come to the first fern hut. It's a little cabinlike house made of cut saplings covered with living ferns and mosses. This was once a small hunting lodge for expeditions from the village into the cloud forest. We're "klostu" our destination now. Our camp, called Wasaunon ("Whasa-EW-non") is nearby. More uphill. Then, a second fern house. Finally, we come to the grassy area dotted with tree ferns. This place is called the kunai ("coon-eye") for the kind of grass it has. Then, a ten-minute walk: Up a slope. Down a slope. Past a big hole. Over slippery logs. Up another muddy trail—and we're "home."

In camp, two other fern houses serve as our combined kitchen and dining room as well as the dormitory for the trackers. They like to sleep by the warm fire inside. They have already erected another series of blue tarps on poles, beneath which we'll pitch our "tent city." We have nine tents—one for each scientist or volunteer. There are two "haus pek pek" or latrines—one for men, another for women. They are also made from saplings and covered with ferns and mosses.

Everything is clothed in moss. The moss is studded with ferns. The ferns are dotted with lichens, liverworts, and fungi. They come in every color, shape, and texture you can imagine. Light green fungi feel like the rubbery ears of a grandfather. Here lichens come in red, and moss can be yellow. Mushrooms look like little umbrellas, or lace, or the icing piped on a birthday cake.

Life piles on life. Fruits and flowers show up where you don't expect them. Figs spring directly from the *trunks* of trees. Whole bushes—rhododendrons with pink and red flowers—grow on tree branches. In a cloud forest, more than three hundred different species of plants might be growing *on a single tree.*

Orchids are everywhere. They perch on branches; they spring from fallen logs; they grow from

ABOVE: Lisa records the day's events in her field notes, at a hand-built camp table. FACING: These magnificent trees are probably well over six hundred years old.

37

tiny cracks in tree bark. Some are as small as a dressmaker's pin. Even the vines are covered with other plants. We can count as many as six species in one square inch of vine. "In just one square foot is a whole little world," says Lisa.

Last year, a botanist tried to count the species of plants here. He quit counting at 117 species, though he plans to resume the count later. It could go on for years.

There may be as many different plants here as in the great rainforests, like the Amazon and the Congo. But unlike those steamy jungles, the cloud forest has few dangers. No jaguars or panthers or piranhas. Few plants have prickers or spines. Mosquitoes are few. It's too cold for snakes (though you find these near villages like Yawan) or crocodiles (which are common in the rivers of New Guinea's lowland rainforests). Everything here seems calm, soft, and safe.

Because there's so much moss—some sitting in big, roundish clumps on the tree branches, with strands of golden vines hanging down like a tail—it can look exactly like the shape and color of a tree kangaroo. "And for years," says Lisa, "that's all we saw up in the trees." Occasional glimpses of her study subject were the best she could hope for—until the year before this expedition.

That's when Lisa, Joel, and Gabriel became the first scientists ever to radio-collar and track wild Matschie's tree kangaroos. They captured and collared three adult females, each with a youngster. Following the signal of the collars with a device that looks like a TV antenna and a receiver that resembles an old-fashioned transistor radio, Joel and Gabriel were able to track them for nearly five months.

"They're probably up in the trees, sitting on their soft cushions of moss right now," says Lisa.

And by six A.M. the next day, one team of trackers is out looking for them. Or for other tree kangaroos no one has met yet.

If the men find any, we'll need a place to keep them until they can be radio-collared and released. Luckily we already have one. Last year, the men made a snug holding cage. It's a fourteen-by-eight-foot enclosure made of sapling-size sticks tied with vines. Ferns, mosses, lichens, and liverworts are growing from its walls—just like the fern huts. "It's actually a living structure," says Lisa, "which makes it even nicer for the tree kangaroos." After a year, it's still in pretty good shape. But it needs some repair.

Christine goes inside the cage to check the climbing perches and walls. She and Lisa decide on the necessary repairs. Like Tom Sawyer and Huck Finn making their river raft, the rest of us begin to gather the materials we need. Joel swings the bush knife to cut ferns to rain-proof the roof. Toby climbs on top to seal the chinks with sticks. Robin strips moss from vines to tie the sticks in place. "It's like building a tree house, only better," says Lisa, "because it's a tree *kangaroo* house." And all the more fun because we do it without hammer or nails.

◦ ◦ ◦

While we were fixing the enclosure, the trackers were hard at work, too. The men split into two teams. One group, led by Gabriel, planned to search along a ridge. Another group was

led by Karau Kuna (we called him Kuna), a twenty-three-year-old research assistant originally from Papua New Guinea's Eastern Highlands. His team would search below the ridge.

By seven A.M., Gabriel's team had found the shoot of a shrub that had clearly been eaten by a tree kangaroo. By noon, they discovered a tree that was covered with scratch marks from a tree kangaroo's claws. Later that afternoon, they visited some of the trees that the radio-collared tree kangaroos sat in last year. Beneath them they found fresh pek pek. But no tree kangaroo.

What they didn't know was what Kuna's team was doing. They had found a tree kangaroo by eight A.M. Joshua spotted one on the ground, standing on its hind legs, feeding on a shrub. Kuna saw it, too. As soon as it saw them, though, the animal hopped away. Joshua took off after it. He might have caught it—if he hadn't tripped over a vine, then fell over a log, and then got a stick caught in his rubber boots.

"We so wanted to get our hands on it!" Joshua explained while Kuna translated. Kuna was just as eager as Joshua. Kuna loves animals. When he was growing up, he had a pet cuscus who used to coil her tail around his ear, and a sugar glider, a marsupial that looks like a flying squirrel, who sailed around the bedroom while he slept. But Kuna had never before seen a wild tree kangaroo.

Joshua, though, has seen many: "Plenti taim mi lukim," he said in Tok Pisin. And then he spoke again through Kuna: "I am happy I saw it today," he said, "and grateful to share it with you. We hope we see more. It's still out there."

FACING: Christine at the tree kangaroo house.

CAPTURE!

"They've got one!"

When we hear the news, we hug one another and leap with excitement. The whole team races down the muddy trail to meet the men at the tree kangaroo house.

"It's a healthy young male," Gabriel announces. He's holding a bulging burlap bag that once contained coffee beans. Today it holds an eighteen-pound Matschie's tree kangaroo. The hunters have named him Ombom, the Tok Ples word people use in Towet for the clumps of moss that look like tree kangaroos.

Ten men had gone searching that morning. They combed the same area where Joshua saw the tree kangaroo the day before. For more than an hour they saw nothing. But then one of them spotted a tree kangaroo about forty feet up in an *Euodia* tree. He called the others. As the men gathered round, the tree kangaroo stared down at them.

Ombom climbed out on a tree limb—then to a smaller branch. And then, he leapt. But unlike most tree kangaroos, Ombom did not land on his feet. He landed on his back.

One of the men tried to hold his head still. Ombom bit him on the finger. Another tracker held Ombom's back legs; Joshua held the front ones. Gabriel came with the coffee bag, and the men lowered Ombom in by his thick golden tail.

So now Lisa looks on while huffing sounds come from the bulge in the burlap. We are all breathless with excitement as Gabriel releases Ombom into the enclosure.

But he's not coming out of the bag. Finally he emerges—slowly. It's dark in the tree kangaroo house, and we peer between the sticks of the cage into the shade. Our hearts sink. Ombom is dragging his left rear leg.

"What's wrong?" asks Lisa.

Our field vet, Holly, isn't sure. The leg could be broken. Ombom could have a nerve injury. Maybe Ombom was sick or injured to start with. That could explain why he landed on his back in the first place.

"I hope I can help," says Holly. But first she needs her anesthesia unit. She needs to put Ombom to sleep to examine him without frightening him.

The anesthetic is a gas delivered by a cone-shaped plastic mask placed over the face. At 2:10 P.M., Holly fits the cone over Ombom's pink nose. As he relaxes, Christine lays him on a silver space blanket on the ground to keep him warm and comfortable.

We all can't help but reach out and touch him. His fur is as soft as a cloud. We all feel just how Gabriel said he felt the first time he held a wild tree kangaroo: "You want to do anything and everything to help them."

Holly moves Ombom's hind leg back and forth gently, testing it. "He doesn't seem to have a fracture," she says.

She gives him a shot of a drug that might reduce swelling around the nerves in his leg. She also gives him a shot of vitamins and minerals. Meanwhile, the trackers gather ferns to make a soft, springy bed in the smallest part of the cage.

"He's doing OK," says Lisa. "His breathing is even."

While he's under, the team takes Ombom's measurements. Scientists use the metric system for recording their data. Tail: 54.5 centimeters (that's a little over 21 inches). Body length: 50.05 centimeters (about 19.5 inches). Holly's thermometer isn't metric. It reads 96.7 Fahrenheit. (Can you convert it to Celsius?) So little is known about wild tree kangaroos that anything we find out is new.

ABOVE: *Wild rhododendron flowers.*
FACING: *Like many cloud forest animals, this jumping spider is probably unknown to science.*

With a special syringe, Holly inserts a tiny microchip beneath his skin. The little chip is only slightly bigger than a grain of rice. It contains a bar code like the one you see on a cereal box, which can be read with a scanner. That way, for the rest of his life, if he is ever captured again, the scientists will know it's him. And then the team puts on Ombum's radio collar. Who knows—maybe he will feel better and be released in a couple of days.

At 3:10 P.M., Ombum starts to wake up.

"There's a good bed of ferns for him?" Lisa asks.

"Yes, yes," answers Gabriel. He lays the animal down on the soft ferns inside the tree kangaroo house so Ombom can wake up in comfort.

As we leave the injured kangaroo in his enclosure, Lisa worries. "I'm torn up about this," Lisa tells us later. "In this kind of work, you don't know what's going to happen. You hate to think an animal might get hurt."

Lisa has thought long and hard about this. "Each individual animal is important," she says. "Each animal has a life, an important life. And the work of a conservation biologist is also to protect many animals, many lives—a whole population.

"I have to think of the big picture," she says. She thinks of the more than 100,000 acres villagers have pledged to protect the tree kangaroos. She thinks about the conservation education programs in Yawan and the other schools—all funded by her research grants. She imagines the thrilling new data each new radio-collared animal might bring—and how such news will help her and her Papuan partners protect the tree kangaroos and their cloud forest even better.

"We are here to protect the habitat for *all* the tree kangaroos," she says. "We want to protect all of them—and this animal is helping us do that."

But still, she worries. "Oh," she says, "I hope he's going to be OK!"

FANTASTIC
CLOUD FORESTS

When is a tropical rainforest not hot and steamy? When it's cool and misty. Then it's a *cloud forest*—a rainforest found only on tropical mountains.

In the cloud forest, warm, humid air from the lowlands rises, cools, and condenses. These special weather conditions create a beautiful, always green forest where the trees grow thick, gnarled, and ancient. Bathed in mist, everything is covered with dense moss, thick ferns, and beautiful orchids.

Cloud forests are rare. Only 2.5 percent of the world's tropical rainforests are cloud forests. There are only a few hundred cloud forests on the planet. Squish them all together and they'd take up less space than Texas. But they're *not* squished together—they're far apart—and that's one thing that makes them places of such rare beauty.

Because cloud forests are often separated from each other by valleys, each cloud forest may have plants and animals found nowhere else. In Peru, one third of the animals who live only in that country call cloud forests their home. In Rwanda, the cloud forest of Mt. Virunga is home to the endangered mountain gorilla. In Costa Rica, the resplendent quetzal, an emerald and scarlet bird with a ribbonlike tail that in males can reach two feet long, migrates between the lowlands and the Monteverde Cloud Forest. Without the cloud forest, it couldn't survive.

And neither would millions of people. Even city dwellers, miles away from cloud forests, depend on them. How? All those ferns and mosses act like a giant sponge. They store water—and that keeps all that water from causing landslides and floods.

In some cities, much of the water that people drink originates in cloud forests. Five million Africans depend on the water from the cloud forests of Mount Kenya. All the water used during the dry season in the Tanzanian capital Dar Es Salaam comes from the cloud forests of the Uluguru Mountains.

It turns out that people need cloud forests as much as animals do.

— *Wild rhododendrons grow high into the canopy. They are one of many foods for Matschie's tree kangaroos.* —

LIFE IN THE BUSH

WE ALL LONG FOR THE MEN TO BRING US MORE TREE KANGA-
ROOS FOR OUR STUDY. BUT ON THE DAYS NO ONE BRINGS TREE
KANGAROOS, THERE'S STILL PLENTY OF WORK TO DO.

"Fieldwork is not just doing science," Lisa explains. "It's also surviving in the bush,
figuring out what foods to eat, charging up the solar batteries, using the Global Positioning System unit. I've learned far more than I ever thought I would."

Even figuring out how to stay warm takes some effort. At night, it's cold and rainy.
We warm up by the smoky fire in the fern huts after dinner. Most of us wear long under-
wear in our sleeping bags. Some wear polar fleece and woolly hats to bed, too. Dry socks
are a must, and unfortunately are becoming a rarity.

Living in the field, we have plenty of chores to do. They might be similar to the chores
you do at home. But here there is no electricity. There are no telephone wires or com-
puters. And everything we use must be carried up on someone's head.

For breakfast, we're not having eggs or toast—eggs would break on the hike up. Bread
would get rained on and grow mold. We make oatmeal instead, or granola with pow-
dered milk. Some of us eat crackers and peanut butter. For lunch we might make instant
soup, just adding boiling water from the tea kettle. For dinner, it's rice, rice, and more
rice. Sometimes we have fresh greens. Sometimes we add lentils, soy sauce, canned fish,
or meat. Once we put ferns in our rice. Sometimes as a special treat we'll have spaghetti.

What about washing the dishes? No dishwasher here. All our washing is done in
the river. Our dishes, our dirty clothes, even our hair. An ice-cold waterfall is our only
shower—so we don't shower very often.

And what about the wet, washed clothes? No dryers. And it's raining more and more
each day. As part of the measurements scientists are always taking, Toby, Joel, and Gabriel
write the figures down daily: A rain gauge tacked to a tree shows that seventy millime-
ters fell in one night. At first we hung our laundry on ropes we strung beneath the tarps
sheltering our tents. But our socks never dried. That's when we started taking our clothes

*ABOVE: James rests in the doorway of an old fern
house once used by hunters. FACING: Evenings are spent
around the fire, swapping stories and cooking.*

47

out to the kunai—the one place with so few trees, it gets really sunny. So up the slippery slope from the washing river, across camp, up another slope, down another, up another muddy trail, we'd carry our wet laundry. And when the clouds would start to gather for more rain? We'd have to rush back out to rescue it.

o o o

All the scientists work hard keeping the equipment dry and ready. On sunny days, Lisa lays out the solar battery panels. They collect the sun's energy to power the batteries in the Global Positioning System units and the satellite telephone she keeps for emergencies. Nic reorganizes his photographic equipment. I write up my notes.

Christine and Holly clean and inventory the veterinary supplies. They check on Ombom and feed him medicine hidden in a banana leaf; we make sure he has fresh bedding and plenty of clean water, and that he is warm and dry in his house.

Robin takes advantage of a lull in the action to mount his climbing gear and explore a huge old tree. He descends with a gorgeous red and yellow orchid. He takes out his watercolors, grinning from ear to ear. "My mentor said this to me about my artwork," Robin tells us. "'If you believe in something, chase it, and chase it as much as you can—you'll be a happy person.' Well," he says, "you can see how happy I am."

o o o

One day, while the trackers are out looking for tree kangaroos, we revisit the area where Lisa and her team caught their first tree kangaroos. They were named Jessie and Shelby—after the two dogs Lisa adopted after her childhood allergies got better (though she never did get over her allergy to cat hair). "They're probably still out there," she says.

Lisa and Joel are taking us to a ridge from which you can see faraway blue mountains—the Sarawaged Range, of which our mountaintop is a part. Along the way, Gabriel names some of the plants for us. *Dacrydium* is the tallest kind of tree, the one in which the tree kangaroos prefer to sit and rest. But though the animals find food in the treetops—orchids, for instance, have been found in their pek pek—the tree kangaroos often eat on the ground, too. They particularly enjoy *Elatostema,* the raspberry-like plant Lisa pointed out as a good sign of tree kangaroo country. And they also love the shoots of the *Saurauia* tree. On the ground, we see its flowers: white petals like a dogwood, with golden centers. It looks like a wedding party has just been through, tossing petals instead of rice.

This place looks like a welcoming living room: A moss-covered log looks like a couch upholstered in green velvet. Mossy stumps resemble matching footstools and easy chairs. The fluffiest moss carpets the forest floor. The vines snaking up the trees look like banisters—for a tree kangaroo staircase. What a beautiful home for Jessie and Shelby!

Lisa remembers the day the team first found them. Everyone had been frustrated. They'd searched for days without success. "This is our land," Dono (the village leader of Yawan) and his nephew, James, said to each other. "Why aren't we

RIGHT: *The tree kangaroos' "living room" is upholstered in green velvet.* FACING, LEFT: *Wild strawberries grow near camp.* FACING, RIGHT: *Saurauia flowers, fallen on moss.*

finding any tree 'roos?" Dono sat beneath a tree, as James looked up into the moss . . . and there he saw a tree kangaroo running over a branch above him.

We're at the base of that tree right now. It's a towering *Dacrydium.* Jessie had jumped out of the tree onto the soft, springy moss below where the men caught her. "It was amazing to watch her jump. She just sort of glided down," Lisa recalls.

Joel and Gabriel located Jessie and Shelby almost every day, recording their observations on a data sheet. Even with the radio collars, the tree kangaroos keep many secrets. "You might not even get to see the whole animal," said Joel, "just a tail or an ear. Sometimes you don't see them at all—but you know they are there because of the radio telemetry."

But knowing where they are is hugely important. From these telemetry recordings, the scientists will be able to see how much land each kangaroo calls home. They'll be able to learn the kangaroos' favorite kinds of trees. "This is how we'll know what habitat needs to be conserved," Lisa says.

After Jessie, two other mothers with joeys were caught, collared, and tracked. The moms were named April (the month she was captured) and Candy (after a friend of Gabriel's). Tracking them revealed important data. The scientists discovered the animals had favorite individual trees—usually a *Dacrydium.* Joel and Gabriel recorded the plants they ate. Sometimes other tree kangaroos were observed in company with the collared animals—sometimes in the same tree. None of this was known before.

Even a tragedy revealed important new information. After

tracking Candy for nearly five months, Joel and Gabriel found her dead one day in August. Her body had been pierced by the curved beak and sharp claws of a giant bird. They're sure it was the New Guinea harpy eagle—the first ever documented attack of a harpy eagle on an adult tree kangaroo.

Of all the new things the scientists found, perhaps this was the most important: For the entire five months, all three mothers stayed in relatively small areas—less than half a kilometer square. April's and Jessie's areas slightly overlapped.

But is this true of all tree kangaroos—or just these three mothers with youngsters? Is the picture different for females with no young? What about youngsters eighteen months old or older, who've just left their moms? And what about the other half of the population—the males? What do *they* do?

We have no idea yet. But with luck we might be able to find out.

MAN NA MERI

Lisa is washing her clothes in the river when we get the news: "Tree 'roos," calls Holly. "*Two* of them!"

One of the trackers has run back to camp to tell us. The two tree kangaroos are "klostu" us—and still up a tree. While Holly and Christine ready the medical equipment, the rest of us race after the tracker to see.

We run past the tree kangaroo house, past the kunai, down a trail—and then into the trackless bush. Will the tree kangaroos still be there when we get there?

It takes us nearly an hour to reach the site. We see the long golden tail hanging down from the branches of a *Saurauia*—and then the animal to whom it belongs: a gorgeous red and gold tree kangaroo sitting eighty feet above us, looking down with ears pricked forward.

"I can't believe it!" Lisa says.

And then, in the tree right next to this tree kangaroo, we see another tail—leading to another tree kangaroo.

"Bigpela pikinini!" one of the trackers exclaims. "Pikinini" is Tok Pisin for child or baby. And "bigpela"? You guessed it: If this is her baby, it's a big one.

ABOVE: *Matschie's tree kangaroo.* FACING: *Cool winds have dwarfed some parts of the forest so it is only abut twenty feet high.*

55

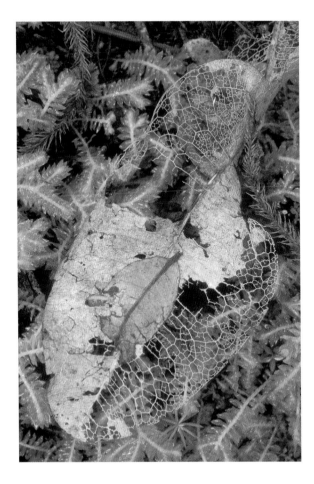

"This is the miracle of doing work here," Lisa says. "They are *so* elusive. And then you finally find them. The whole field season is riding on these moments."

o o o

The men had left camp that morning feeling lucky. "It was sunny and warm," Gabriel recalled. "A good day for the tree 'roos to come out and warm themselves." They changed their strategy: "For the first three days, we were traveling more than one kilometer each day to find tree 'roos. I had wanted our presence to drive them closer to camp. So we decided today to try closer—and it worked."

The men spread out. One tracker decided he would look for a plant that the tree kangaroos love to eat. It grows high on tree branches and is easy to spot. The underside is brown and the top green. He found one in a tree—but no tree kangaroo. He scanned the next tree over—the *Saurauia*—and there was the tail!

"Immediately," the tracker explained through Gabriel, "I barked like a dog because that would keep her up in the tree. Everyone else heard the barking and knew what happened. Everyone ran and admired the 'roo. We all stood looking for about two minutes. And then someone noticed there was another tail."

o o o

We photograph and videotape and watch the two tree kangaroos for ten minutes. Now to get the animals down . . .

The trackers have been thinking about this puzzle. Shortly after they spotted the animals, they began to cut sticks and brush to build a low fence they call an "im" around the tree. If the tree kangaroo leaps down and starts to hop away, the im will slow him down.

One of the trackers takes off his tall rubber boots. Barefoot, he begins to climb a smaller tree next to the *Saurauia.* Within two minutes, he's as high as the tree kangaroo.

"Joel, do you see where she is?" asks Lisa. Joel has the 'roo in his binoculars. "She's still there," he assures.

But the tree kangaroo isn't happy to see a human approaching. She climbs another 30 feet up to get away. If she jumps, it's a 110-foot drop.

Suddenly, she leaps, her forearms outstretched. She drops 30 feet. She grabs a smaller tree on the way down. And now she begins to back down the tree.

She's almost to the ground when one of the trackers grabs her by the tail and puts her in the burlap bag.

"Pikinini! Pikinini!" the men call. The other tree kangaroo is 65 feet up in the *Decaspermum* tree, and they don't want him to get away. The tree kangaroo lets go of the branch. Like an acrobat, he catches a vine with his front paws, turns himself around, and lands on the ground on his feet. One tracker holds the chest, another holds the back legs, and another man holds the front.

It's only now that we realize that the "baby" is a fully grown adult male. "Man na meri" the trackers say—this pair is no mother and baby, but a grown-up male and female on a tree kangaroo date. By 10:10 A.M., both tree kangaroos are in burlap bags, heading back to camp.

o o o

Twenty-five minutes later, we're all back in camp, where Holly and Christine have set up the exam table—a picnic table built from saplings lashed with vines. They've laid out medical supplies and sample vials, measuring tools and data sheets. Each tree kangaroo will be given medicine to make it sleep while the team puts on the radio collar and conducts a health exam.

We want to find out as much as we can. Because so little is known about tree kangaroos, every detail is important.

First, while the animals are in their burlap bags, they are weighed. The female weighs 6.4 kilograms (about 24 pounds)

Once an animal has been seen, a tracker climbs a nearby tree to scare it into coming down.

with the bag. The scientists will make sure to subtract the weight of the bag alone later. The male, with bag, weighs 8 kilograms.

Joel notes the temperature and humidity, too: It's 56.2 degrees Fahrenheit, 81 percent humidity.

"Let's measure the male's neck, to make sure the radio collar will fit on him," says Lisa. "But let's do the female first."

"With the female, we'll have the same priorities," Holly tells the group. "We'll measure the neck, put on the radio collar, insert the ID chip, pluck fur for more testing, check the pouch—see if she has a baby."

We hope to find out as much as we can while the animal is asleep. But anesthesia can be dangerous. That's why we'll be carefully watching how often she breathes in and out and how fast her heart is beating during the procedure. We'll have to work fast. Everyone will help.

"Christine will call out pulse and respiration every five minutes," says Holly. "Is everybody ready?"

"Do you have the radio collar?" Lisa asks Gabriel.

Gabriel is holding a leather collar much like one a dog might wear. Instead of metal tags, though, it has a little box of waterproof plastic. This contains a transmitter powered by a square battery and outfitted with an internal antenna. Each radio collar also has a computer chip. Without knowing it, the tree kangaroos will be sending their position not only to the scientists tracking them on the ground, but also to satellites circling thousands of miles above Earth. At six A.M. and six P.M. —times the 'roos are likely to be in the trees and the weather is likely to be less cloudy—the satellites read the animals' exact position on the earth's surface. They download this informa-

A Matschie's looks down from eighty feet up in the canopy.

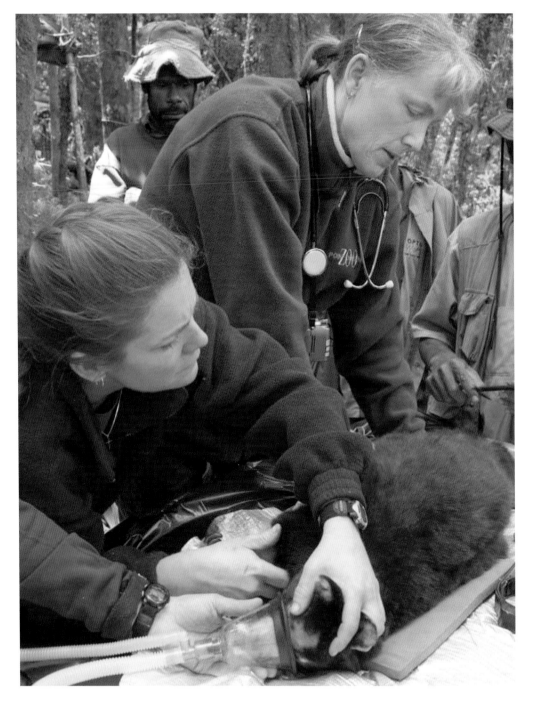

tion to the chips in the collars, and this data can be transferred to a computer when the collar automatically falls off, after five months. The whole thing weighs less than half a pound.

"Do you have the screwdriver to put the collar on?" asks Lisa.

"Yes, yes," says Gabriel, holding the squirming bag on his lap. "We're ready!"

But the tree kangaroo isn't. Gabriel talks to the animal in the bag. "Wait, wait, come here," he says gently. And then, to two trackers: "Hold 'im!" Soon a pink nose pokes out through a hole in the bag.

It's 10:55 A.M. and Holly places the mask on the nose. A paw comes out through the hole. But within forty-five seconds, the tree kangaroo relaxes. The anesthesia's working. She's asleep.

Out comes the kangaroo. "Thermometer?" Holly requests.

The kangaroo's body temperature is similar to a person's: 97.1 degrees.

"Respiration is thirty-two," says Christine. That means she's breathing thirty-two times a minute. That's healthy.

Holly leans forward to listen to the heart through her stethoscope. For five seconds, she counts the beats. She wants to calculate the beats per minute. "Heart rate is sixteen times twelve. You do the math," she tells Joel, who is recording everything on a data sheet.

Meanwhile, Gabriel is putting on the collar. "Make sure the collar is comfortable but snug," says Lisa. (Yesterday Christine discovered that Ombum had taken his off and left it on the floor of his cage.)

The team works fast while the tree kangaroo is anesthetized.

Holly puts in the microchip and Joel records its number: 029-274-864.

"I'm going to do a pouch check," says Holly. Meanwhile, the other scientists measure everything they can as fast as they can.

"Pouch is empty," says Holly. "Now for the vitamin-mineral shot."

"This is it," says Lisa. She calls an end to the exam. Because he was injured, Ombum's exam took much longer; but we don't want to subject this tree kangaroo to the anesthesia any longer than necessary, for safety's sake.

Holly removes the face mask and quickly checks the teeth. She's coming to. It's 11:06 A.M.

"Put her in the bag," says Lisa. "Tail first, so she can sit." They name her Tess, in honor of my dog, a Border collie who died last year at age sixteen. The new Tess rests in her bag on a tracker's lap while we prepare for the male.

○ ○ ○

11:20 A.M.: "Anesthetic machine? Gas ready? Radio collar?" Holly asks. "And is the other 'roo OK?"

"OK," answers the team. "We're ready!"

Each radio collar allows scientists to track a tree kangaroo for several months.

Gabriel unties the top of the male's bag, and immediately the burlap boils with movement.

"He's doing somersaults in the bag," Gabriel reports. It's all he and Joshua can do to hold the 'roo.

Through the bag, the male grabs one man's glove and pulls it off. He bites another tracker on the finger. Now four men are struggling. "I've got his head here," says Gabriel, "but I can't get it out—but the nose is right here!"

Through the burlap, Holly delivers the anesthetic. "Oh, but he's tough!" says Gabriel.

Finally the bag stops wiggling. At 11:30 A.M. the male is lifted out of the bag and laid out on the table. The team goes to work.

"Seventeen times twelve is the heart rate," Holly tells Joel.

"Twenty-two point seven, circumference of neck," says Toby. "Here's the collar. Let's put it on."

"Respiration is twenty," says Holly. "Now we'll take his temperature. Next the chip. And after that we'll go for the hair."

Everything is going like clockwork. Then Christine warns, "Respiration slowing . . ."

"That's it. Let's pull the mask off," says Lisa.

It's 11:37 A.M. "His ears are twitching. Let's get him back in the bag," says Holly.

It's all over in just ten minutes. "Great work," says Lisa.

○ ○ ○

Noon. We're at the tree kangaroo house. The men have cut fern fronds and lined the two apartments inside with this soft, moist carpet. They've used ferns to screen the wall between the new pair and Ombum, so the animals won't upset each other. Ombum looks calm. Though his leg is no better, he is now taking banana leaves from Christine's hands.

We all sit quietly while one of the trackers opens the cage door. Tess climbs out of the bag and scurries up a perch. She regards us with interest, but no fear. Lisa has named the male Christopher—in honor of my pig, who grew to 750 pounds and lived to age fourteen. The kangaroo Christopher rushes out of his bag and climbs to the highest perch.

Joel and Gabriel want to make sure the collars are working, so they have brought their radio receivers along to check. Each animal has its own frequency, almost like a phone number. If Joel wants to tune in to Tess, he dials up channel 151.080. Christopher's channel is 150.050. Both collars work fine.

We're all delighted. One tracker is so enthusiastic, he wants to go out and hunt for more tree kangaroos this very afternoon. "But the hotel is full!" says Lisa. The cage has all the tree kangaroos it can hold.

We all shake hands, hug, and smile. Everyone is beaming with a mixture of excitement, exhaustion—and relief.

"The first collared male Matschie's tree kangaroo," says Gabriel. "History!"

THE CRUCIAL TEST

FROM NIGHT AFTER NIGHT OF RAIN, THE TRAILS AROUND CAMP ARE EXTRA SLIPPERY. OUR BOOTS ARE SO CAKED WITH MUD THAT EACH MUST WEIGH AN EXTRA POUND. BUT WE don't mind. Our hearts are light—because the morning after their capture, we are going to release the two tree kangaroos.

Joshua leads the procession to the capture site, carrying Tess in a burlap bag. The release goes perfectly: Tess pops out of her bag and scurries up a tree. Chris follows. Within seconds, the pair of tree kangaroos are completely hidden by leaves.

"You release two tree kangaroos into a tree, and where are they?" asks Lisa. "Isn't it incredible how they just disappear?"

It's easy to see why we'll need the telemetry to ever find them again.

We leave the pair alone to get resettled in their forest home. Everything has gone remarkably well so far. But the next day will be critical. That's when we'll return to this site for the crucial test of the expedition. Can we find the tree kangaroos again with our telemetry? If we can't, we will have collared these animals for nothing. But if we can, we will really make history—and prove what some scientists said was impossible really *can* be done.

o o o

We reach the release site at 7:35 A.M. Joel unfolds the telemetry antenna. He tries to dial up Tess's channel on the receiver. Nothing. Then he switches to Christopher's. Beep, beep, beep comes the answer. But it is faint. Christopher could be far away.

Joel waves the antenna like a magician's wand. And it does seem as if we need some magic. Will we be able to find an invisible tree kangaroo?

— *ABOVE: Lisa heads to the release site.* *FACING: The dense canopy of vines and mossy branches makes it almost impossible to find tree kangaroos.* —

65

The rest of us scan the trees with binoculars. "I think I see him!" Lisa cries. She points to the tree in which the pair were released. We all strain to see.

"False alarm," she says. "Sorry. That vine looks just like a tail."

Joel swings the antenna. The high-pitched beeping seems to deepen.

"Klostu," says Gabriel.

We head down slope, into a little valley thick with waist-high herbs. Gabriel moves ahead with his bush knife, cutting a path.

Then, uphill. Every path is steep, and this can distort the radio signal. The signal can bounce off ridges, even trees. It can seem as though the tree kangaroo is close when he's really far—or in one direction when he's actually in another.

Beep, beep, beep. The signal seems to be getting fainter, not stronger. But at 8:05 A.M., we hear a new sound in the distance. It sounds like . . . barking. But there are no dogs here.

It takes a moment before we realize one of the trackers is barking like a dog. And there's only one reason he would do that. "They've already found a new tree kangaroo!" exclaims Lisa.

Joel and Gabriel move ahead, following the signal. The rest of us trail them up a ridge. We stop to scan the treetops.

Where is Christopher?

Beep, beep, beep. Down and up we go. Slipping, falling, tripping. Although it's still cool out, we're so warm from our hike, we tie our polar fleeces around our waists.

"This is really intense work," says Lisa. "This really challenges you on so many different levels. Look at everything we have to do: We're hacking through the bush. We're radio-tracking. This is so different from science in the laboratory, isn't it?

"My guess is, he took off the minute we left yesterday," says Lisa. "But

with males, we have no idea. We don't know how far they range. This is all new information."

Beep, beep, beep.

Then, at 9:07 A.M., the signal swells.

"He's in a tree!" cries Gabriel.

"Yes—but which one?"

"This way—over the ridge."

"Somewhere here, he's hiding."

We've climbed up a 60-degree slope to a knife-edge ridge. We're right across from a particularly magnificent mountain cedar. It's a great castle of a tree, full of hollows, laced with vines, and draped with moss. Along one side, the moss has parted. Inch-long gashes show where someone's strong claws gripped the tree's bark. Christopher must have climbed this tree this morning.

But finding him "is like looking for a needle in a haystack," says Lisa. "Except it's a whole farm full of haystacks. But we have a little beep to help us."

The signal's really clear now. Joel is pointing the antenna up at a 40-degree angle. We all scan the tree with our binoculars.

"I see him!" Gabriel shouts. "He's looking right at us!"

"Yes," says Lisa. "It *is* Christopher!"

Now it's time to take more measurements. Even though we're not in a laboratory, we're still on the cutting edge of science. Gabriel, Joel, and Toby unpack the equipment from their backpacks: A clinometer tells us that from where we stand to the top of the tree is an angle of 40 degrees, and that Christopher is at an angle of 29 degrees from where Gabriel is standing. A rangefinder tells us we are seventeen meters away from Christopher's tree. The Global Positioning System unit tells us precisely where we are standing in degrees, minutes, and seconds—as well as our elevation (2,877) in meters.

Joel and Gabriel also measure the slope (65 degrees) and the temperature (14.4 degrees Celsius). Then Gabriel decides, just for fun, to try dialing up Tess's channel again. He sets the receiver on 151.080.

The answer is loud and immediate: BEEP, BEEP, BEEP.

"It's Tess." Gabriel is amazed. "They're together!"

Never have any scientists been able to follow two tree kangaroos on a date before. No one ever knew how long a male and female might stay near each other. "We are seeing totally new science here," says Lisa.

For forty-five minutes, we wander about, trying to see Tess. But all we ever find is more claw marks at the base of a neighboring tree—a tree even bigger than Christopher's, with a crown larger than most backyards.

Finally, it begins to rain. No chance of *seeing* Tess today—but we've found her nonetheless. "She's probably watching us now," says Lisa. "You can see why people said it was too hard to study tree kangaroos."

But Lisa and her team have proved them wrong—for the second year in a row. We've had a very successful day. And when we get back to camp, a surprise is waiting.

o o o

The barking we heard signaled even better news than we thought. The trackers didn't find just one new tree kangaroo—they found *two*.

The new pair will be another first for the study: a mother and her nearly grown son. Lisa estimates that he's fifteen months old—nearly old enough to leave his mother. But what do the young males do when they leave their moms? Many young male animals travel far away at this point in their lives.

RIGHT: Joey, a young male, is an exciting find for the team. FACING: Many hands gently restrain, reassure, and measure Joey before his radio collar is attached.

70

How about tree kangaroos? Nobody knows.

This fellow may well be the first young male tree kangaroo in history to be tracked during this very critical phase of his life. Gabriel names the youngster Joey—after Joel. Lisa names Joey's mother Holly, in honor of our field vet.

The radio-collaring and measurements go smoothly. In fact, Joey is so calm, he needs no anesthetic at all. He stays wide-eyed and still while we all hold him and pet him. Who can resist gently rubbing that lemon yellow tummy?

In just a few days, Lisa and most of the team will be leaving. Toby, Gabriel, Kuna, and a number of the trackers will stay, following the animals every day to discover what these four tree kangaroos have to teach us.

We are all so grateful for the incredible luck we've had so far. We're grateful to our Papuan friends for all their hard work and kind help. But most of all, we're grateful to the tree kangaroos —for their endearing beauty and for their mystery, and for the opportunity to learn some of their secrets for the first time.

Lisa speaks softly to Joey as we take our measurements and put on his collar. "Good boy," she says, her voice mixing tenderness with awe. "So good!"

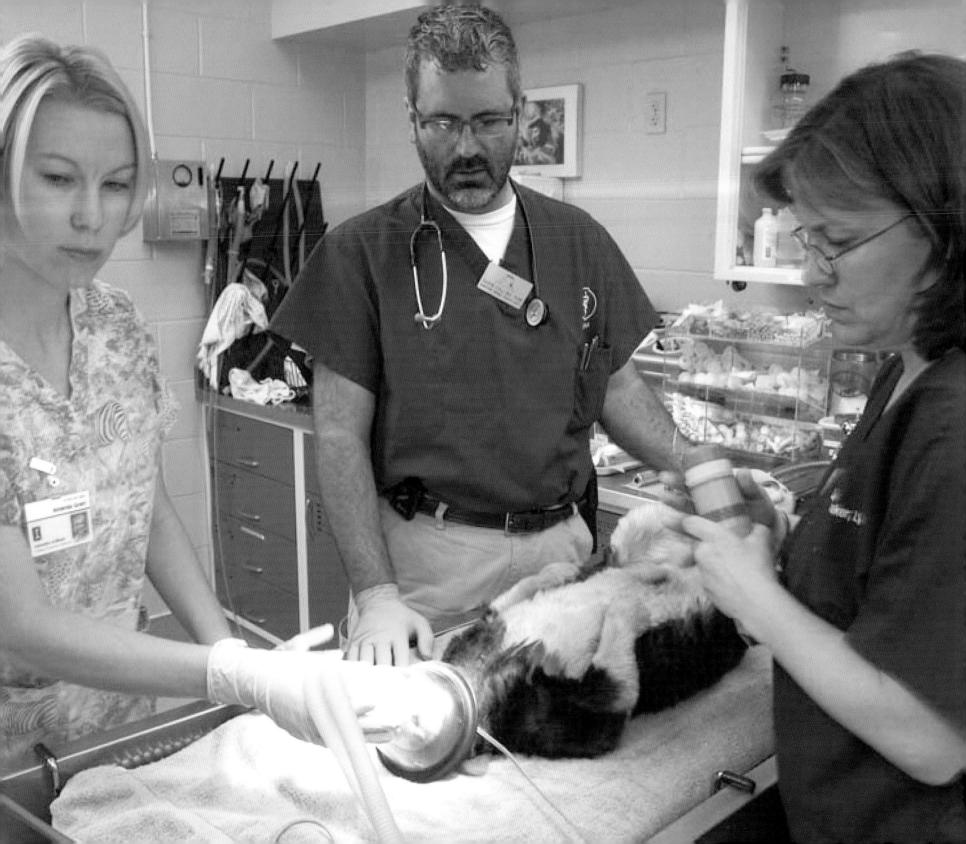

CONSERVATION AT HOME— AND AROUND THE WORLD

JIRRAH, A THIRTEEN-YEAR-OLD FEMALE MATSCHIE'S TREE KANGAROO, IS LYING COMFORTABLY ASLEEP ON THE EXAMINATION TABLE IN THE SURGICAL SUITE OF WOODLAND PARK ZOO. SHE'S IN FOR HER ANNUAL HEALTH CHECK.

What a difference from our makeshift clinic in the field. Illuminated by bright fluorescent lights, the surgical suite is modern and spotless. Everything is neatly in its place: needles and swabs, syringes and gloves, disinfectant and bandages. If needed, machines stand by to suction clogged airways or shock a stopped heart back to life. A pulse oximeter records Jirrah's heart rate and the amount of oxygen in her blood. If there's a problem, it automatically sounds a shrill alarm.

As Lisa looks on, veterinarian Darin Collins, the director of the zoo's animal health department, checks many of the same things Holly did for the wild tree kangaroos in the field. He gently examines Jirrah's pouch, her teeth, her eyes, her ears, and her claws. He weighs her (a big girl at 9.35 kilogram). Darin takes a blood sample. But here at the zoo, he can do more: He takes X-rays. He takes a throat culture. "We take this very seriously," says the veterinarian. "Jirrah's very important to us. All our animals are."

Just like Lisa, Darin believes that every individual animal matters—whether in the wild or in the zoo. Each matters for the same reasons we do: Each loves its life. Each deserves a chance to be happy, healthy, and comfortable. But some of us—like Lisa and like Jirrah—have a larger calling, too.

"What *is* it?" asks a teenager in a pink T-shirt. "Is it a koala bear? It has a pouch!"

o o o

"It's a *tree kangaroo*," a nine-year-old reads off the exhibit tag. "It lives in *trees*."

As always, there's a crowd gathering around Jirrah, now fully recovered from her exam and back in her exhibit with her male companion, Wewak.

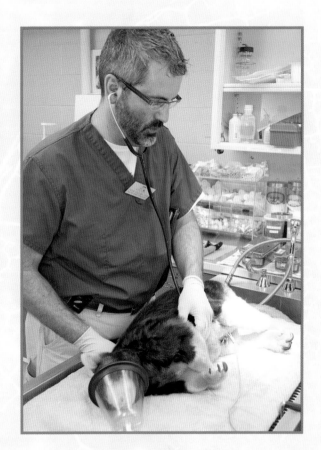

— HERE AND FACING: At Woodland Park Zoo, Darin performs an annual physical checkup on Jirrah the tree kangaroo. —

LISA'S ADVICE FOR KIDS

It all boils down to three words, says Lisa: "Follow your passion!" It doesn't matter where you live. It doesn't matter if friends or teachers don't always understand. And it doesn't matter if you have a physical challenge like asthma. "With asthma," Lisa says, "sure, you have to take care of it. But it doesn't have to stop you."

If your passion is wild animals and wild places, here are some of Lisa's suggestions:

1. Learn more about your favorite animals. Read books and magazines at the library. Search the Internet. Watch shows on TV. But be sure to spend time watching animals firsthand—at the zoo, in your yard, wherever you can.

2. Find out what's happening in your favorite animal's home. If the animal lives in the sea, is pollution a problem? If it's a forest animal, are the trees being cut down?

3. You can help. Join a beach cleanup. Write letters to the editor at your local paper. Urge leaders to pass laws protecting wild animals and wild lands. Even the foods you eat, the car your family drives, and the toys and clothes you select can affect animals' lives. Share with others what you've found out and how they can help.

4. In your backyard, plant gardens to attract birds and butterflies and other animals, to create better homes for them. When you recycle aluminum, cardboard, and plastic, you help animals by keeping garbage from littering their homes.

5. Join an organization like Rainforest Conservation Fund, Conservation International, or Wildlife Conservation Society. There are many other excellent groups doing good work around the world to protect animals and their homes. Become a member of your local zoo, aquarium, or natural history museum.

And in the future? What if you want to make a life helping animals, like Lisa does? Lisa advises, "You can study hard in school. For me, it was learning the sciences and math, which I liked. But wildlife is interdisciplinary. That means it's science, but also art, and also politics.

"Some people help by being teachers," she explains. "Some people help by becoming biologists, or artists, or politicians. It takes a lot of different kinds of people to help conserve wildlife —and we need them all!"

"Grandma, look—it's so cute!" calls a younger child. "Kangaroos that live in *trees!*"

"They're so cute hunched over like that," says an older woman wearing a shirt showing an American flag shaped like a heart. "They look like they're praying."

Almost everyone who sees them can't wait to show their companions: *"Look!"*

And that's just what Lisa hopes people will do. "There's nothing more inspiring than seeing a tree kangaroo up close," she says. "To know one is to love one. They're so endearing. They are truly the ambassadors for their wild cousins. When people see them eat, watch them move, see what they do, they'll want to help them."

Jirrah is one of those ambassador animals. Like Lisa, she's helping to save tree kangaroos—even though her wild cousins are on the opposite side of the world.

∘ ∘ ∘

It's been more than two months since Lisa returned from the field. Toby and Gabriel have called on the satellite phone with updates on the wild tree kangaroos: Christopher's travels have taken him all over the map. Tess's, too —in fact, they lost track of her for a week until she showed up again, close to camp. Holly and Joey, though, seem to be staying in a nice stable home range. At least for the moment.

Unfortunately, Ombom never got to join them. To everyone's sorrow, and despite the best care we could give, he died just before Lisa had to leave. Veterinarian Holly

believes he had probably suffered brain or nerve damage when he was a joey, possibly from an earlier fall from a tree. He was probably quite sick before we ever caught him. He lies buried at Wasaunon. None of us will ever forget him.

o o o

Even while she's working at the zoo, the wild tree kangaroos of New Guinea are never far from Lisa's thoughts. She supports her research team in the field by making sure they have what they need. "I have to spend time writing reports, raising money, trying to get other people to support what we do," she explains.

Twenty-five other North American zoos, and a number of larger conservation organizations, including Conservation International, support the Tree Kangaroo Conservation Program. And as conservation director at the Woodland Park Zoo, Lisa is also working to expand partnerships with other groups and other projects: One is the International Snow Leopard Trust. Another project helps conserve the endangered Siberian cranes of Russia.

No matter whether she's in Papua New Guinea or in Seattle, Washington, whether she's climbing a mountain or at the zoo, Lisa is working to help—by making people care.

TREE KANGAROOS
NEAR YOU

More than two dozen U.S. zoos, and several in Canada, have tree kangaroos you can visit! To find the 200 nearest you, visit *WWW.AZA.ORG* and select "AZA Zoos & Aquariums," then select your state.

To learn more:

○ What's the latest news of Lisa's study? What are the kids in Yawan doing in class? To find out, visit Woodland Park Zoo's Web site, *WWW.ZOO.ORG* or *WWW.TREEKANGAROO.ORG*. You'll see new photos from the field, too.

○ Read about a woman who raises orphaned tree kangaroos. Learn how gorillas helped Joel get to Papua New Guinea. Find out how Kuna got his tribal tattoo. For these stories as well as translations of interviews with native trackers working for the Tree Kangaroo Conservation Program, visit *WWW.AUTHORWIRE.COM*.

○ Dreaming of a trip to Australia or Papua New Guinea? Even there, tree kangaroos can be hard to find in the wild. But you can still get up close and personal—here's how:

• Visit Australian zoos with tree kangaroos. To get addresses, visit *WWW.ARAZPA.ORG*.

• Stay at an Australian tree kangaroo sanctuary. Lumholtz Lodge, set amid 160 acres of Queensland rainforest, is run by wildlife rehabilitator Margit Cianelli. Her specialty? Raising orphaned baby tree kangaroos! Visit via the Web page at *WWW.USERS.BIGPOND.COM/LUMHOLTZLODGE* or e-mail her at *LUMHOLTZLODGE@YAHOO.COM.AU*.

• The Rainforest Habitat in Lae, Papua New Guinea, has 4 kinds of tree kangaroos—more species of tree kangaroo than any other zoo in the world. It's also got more than 30 species of unique birds, including cassowaries and birds of paradise, 10,000 native plants, and forest wallabies, flying foxes, crocodiles, and incredible butterflies. You can send e-mail to find out more at *INFO.HABITAT@GLOBAL.ORG.PG*

○ Teachers: Want your class to correspond with kids in Papua New Guinea? To arrange this—or to join the International Bug Club network, or an international art exchange—write the webmaster at *WWW.ZOO.ORG* at the Woodland Park Zoo.

LET'S TOK PISIN

Tok Pisin is a real language—not a dialect or a kind of "broken" English. But many of its words come from English roots (the same way that many English words come from German or French roots). See if you can recognize some of them below.

Words:

APINUN—good afternoon

BAGARAP—broken or worn out

BIGPELA—big

BILAK—black

DOKTA—doctor

HAUS—house

HAUS PEK PEK—toilet or latrine

KLOSTU—nearby or close to

KUNAI—open area or grassland

LIK-LIK—little

LONGWE—far away

LUKAUT—watch out, beware of

NOGAT—no

NOGUT—bad

PAITIM—hit

RAITIM—write

SAVE—know

SINGAUT—to call out

SU—shoe or shoes

TIME—time

WASWAS—bathe

Phrases:

SAMPELA BILAK BOKIS NA SPOS YU PAITIM TEE BILONG EM I SINGAUT

—(Here's a hint: "Some kind of black box—suppose you hit its teeth? It calls out." And another: it's a big, heavy musical instrument.)

PIK I KAIKAI SU BILONG EM.

—The pig ate his shoes.

MURUK I BAI KAM LONG BUS BILONG YUMI.

—The cassowary is coming to our forest ("the bush belonging to you, me").

MI LIKIM KAPUL LONGPELA TEL!

—I like tree kangaroos!

ACKNOWLEDGMENTS: TENK YU TRU

Like studying tree kangaroos, creating this book called upon the wisdom and kindness of many people and animals. In addition to the individuals you've met on these pages, we'd especially like to thank Deborah Jensen, Gai Kula, Ginson Saonu, Judie Steenberg, Governor Luther Wenge, John Williar, YUS Local Level Government, the staff of the Tree Kangaroo Conservation Program, the Huon Peninsula communities where Lisa works, the Roger Williams Park Zoo, the Woodland Park Zoo, and the other AZA Tree Kangaroo Species Survival Plan zoos. We also thank Margit Cianelli at Lumholtz Lodge and the staff of Rainforest Habitat, where some of the photographs in this book were taken.

— We would like to thank our trackers and guides for their patience, kindness, and great humor. —

INDEX

Page numbers in *italics* refer to photographs or
    drawings.

° A Note from the Author

Because of the kind of books I write, I've had to contend with obstacles few authors face if they stay sensibly home at their desks. Once, in Borneo, an orangutan ate my interview tapes. In India, while I was riding an elephant, my notebook fell out of my backpack (the elephant picked it up with her trunk and gave it back to me). On other projects, I've had to hike for days and swim for miles. But going to New Guinea was my most physically strenuous expedition of all . . . so far.

Although I never once considered quitting, during the second day's hike to the field site, I quietly wondered whether I was having a nine-hour heart attack. I gasped for every breath. My heart banged so hard in my chest, I thought it would knock me over. Though I am physically pretty fit, I probably had altitude sickness, which can strike anyone—and the faulty valve in my heart probably didn't help. When we reached our first campsite, I threw up from exhaustion. Nic found me wandering around without my jacket in the rain, my lips blue from cold. I knew something was wrong but was too sick to realize what to do. But Nic knew: he stuffed me into Lisa's tent, where I could get warm. Everyone took such good care of me that night, I was never frightened.

It's no wonder I felt so safe and cared for: I was among friends. Nic and I had worked together on two previous books, which took us to a pit swarming with 18,000 snakes and to the jungles of French Guiana to meet tarantulas. I love working with him. I'd known and admired Lisa for five years. I had known Joel—to whom I dedicated this book—since he was in the ninth grade, back when an expedition like this seemed to him a far-off dream. Very quickly, though, *all* the members of the expedition became like family to me. That's why they named two tree kangaroos after pets of mine who had died the year before—they knew just how much that would heal my broken heart. Which it did. I hope to stay friends with the folks on our team forever.

—S.M.

° A Note from the Photographer

I did a lot of planning for this expedition. I knew there would be nowhere to buy spare film once I got to the cloud forest, or any power outlets to recharge my camera batteries. So I had to carefully make a list of all the photo equipment I would need for three weeks. This included several cameras and lenses, four flash guns, a tripod, some flash stands, memory cards for my digital camera, sixty rolls of film, about a hundred batteries, an umbrella to keep my camera dry while I was taking photos, plastic bags to keep it dry while it was in my pack, and dozens of cables, connectors, spare parts, and other important bits.

Then there was the next problem: my camera stuff weighed about twenty-five pounds and I was going to have to carry it—all the time. After all, I never knew when I might see something I wanted to photograph. But I didn't want to hold the others up and I couldn't afford to get tired. I would have to work hard every day to get all the photographs I wanted for this book in just three weeks, and there would be no second chances if I made mistakes. So I did a lot of training to get fit, taking long cross-country runs throughout Michigan's snowy winter.

In the end everything worked out well. It was the most exciting and busy three weeks of photography in my life, although I probably lost several pounds of body weight. A big highlight was finding out that I still remembered much of the Tok Pisin I had learned as a teenager living in Papua New Guinea. It was fun to sit around the fire at night with the trackers and swap funny stories about things that had happened in our lives.

—N.B.

www.hmhbooks.com

The text of this book is set in Angie.

The Library of Congress has catalogued the hardcover edition as follows:

Montgomery, Sy.
Quest for the tree kangaroo / written by Sy Montgomery ; with photographs by Nic Bishop.
p. cm.
1. Matschie's tree kangaroo—Juvenile literature. 2. Dabek, Lisa.
I. Bishop, Nic, 1955– II. Title.
QL737.M35M66 2006
599.2'2—dc22
2005034849

ISBN: 978-0-547-24892-9 pb

Manufactured in China
SCP 10 9
4500421869
Maps on pages 4 and 5 © Robin Wingrave
Page 8: William Betz
Page 80: Lisa Dabek